HOW DOES IT WORK?

TVs AND REMOTE CONTROLS

by Nikole Brooks Bethea

pogo

Ideas for Parents and Teachers

Pogo Books let children practice reading informational text while introducing them to nonfiction features such as headings, labels, sidebars, maps, and diagrams, as well as a table of contents, glossary, and index.

Carefully leveled text with a strong photo match offers early fluent readers the support they need to succeed.

Before Reading

- "Walk" through the book and point out the various nonfiction features. Ask the student what purpose each feature serves.
- Look at the glossary together. Read and discuss the words.

Read the Book

- Have the child read the book independently.
- Invite him or her to list questions that arise from reading.

After Reading

- Discuss the child's questions. Talk about how he or she might find answers to those questions.
- Prompt the child to think more. Ask: Did you know how TVs worked before reading this book? What more would you like to learn about TV and remote control technology?

Pogo Books are published by Jump!
5357 Penn Avenue South
Minneapolis, MN 55419
www.jumplibrary.com

Library of Congress Cataloging-in-Publication Data

Names: Bethea, Nikole Brooks, author.
Title: TVs and remote controls / by Nikole Brooks Bethea. Description: Minneapolis: Jump!, Inc., [2021]
Series: How does it work?
Includes index. Audience: Ages 7-10.
Identifiers: LCCN 2020033550 (print)
LCCN 2020033551 (ebook)
ISBN 9781645277927 (hardcover)
ISBN 9781645277934 (paperback)
ISBN 9781645277941 (ebook)
Subjects: LCSH: Television–Receivers and reception Juvenile literature. Television–Tuners–Juvenile literature. | Remote control–Juvenile literature.
Classification: LCC TK6640 .B46 2021 (print)
LCC TK6640 (ebook) | DDC 621.388/8–dc23
LC record available at https://lccn.loc.gov/2020033550
LC ebook record available at https://lccn.loc.gov/2020033551

Editor: Eliza Leahy
Designer: Molly Ballanger

Photo Credits: Ruslan Ivantsov/Shutterstock, cover (tv), 4 (tv); oraveepix/Shutterstock, cover (remote); manaemedia/Shutterstock, 1; Vladimir Sukhachev/Shutterstock, 3; ben bryant/Shutterstock, 4 (boy); PhotoStock10/Shutterstock, 4 (screen); 9comeback/Shutterstock, 5; Nick Starichenko/Shutterstock, 6-7; Suradech Prapairat/Shutterstock, 8; Vladimir Stanisic/Dreamstime, 9 (background); Oleksiy Mark/Shutterstock, 9 (tv screen); Classic Picture Library/SuperStock, 10-11; Germain McDaniel/Shutterstock, 12-13; Early Spring/Shutterstock, 14-15 (background); wavebreakmedia/Shutterstock, 14-15 (tv screen); Wavebreakmedia Ltd/Dreamstime, 16-17; lunamarina/Shutterstock, 16-17 (tv screen); gallofoto/Shutterstock, 18; Andrey_Popov/Shutterstock, 19; Photo-SD/Shutterstock, 19 (tv screen); FrameStockFootages/Shutterstock, 20-21; LesPalenik/Shutterstock, 23.

Printed in the United States of America at Corporate Graphics in North Mankato, Minnesota.

TABLE OF CONTENTS

CHAPTER 1

HOW TVs WORK

Do you watch television? Have you ever wondered how your favorite shows play?

Transmitters at TV stations send **signals**. They travel through the air as **radio waves**. They show up on your TV as pictures. The sound travels the same way.

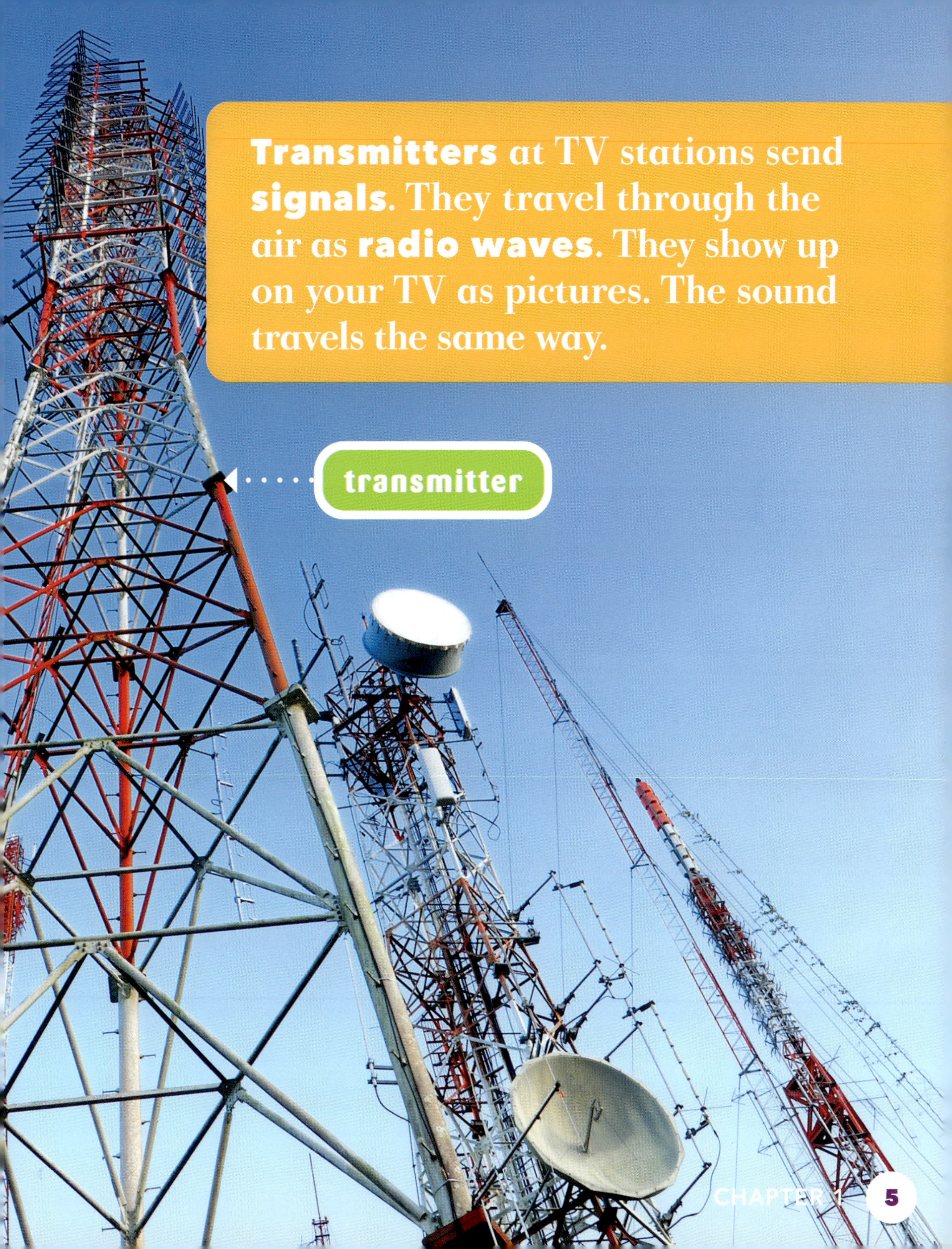

satellite dish

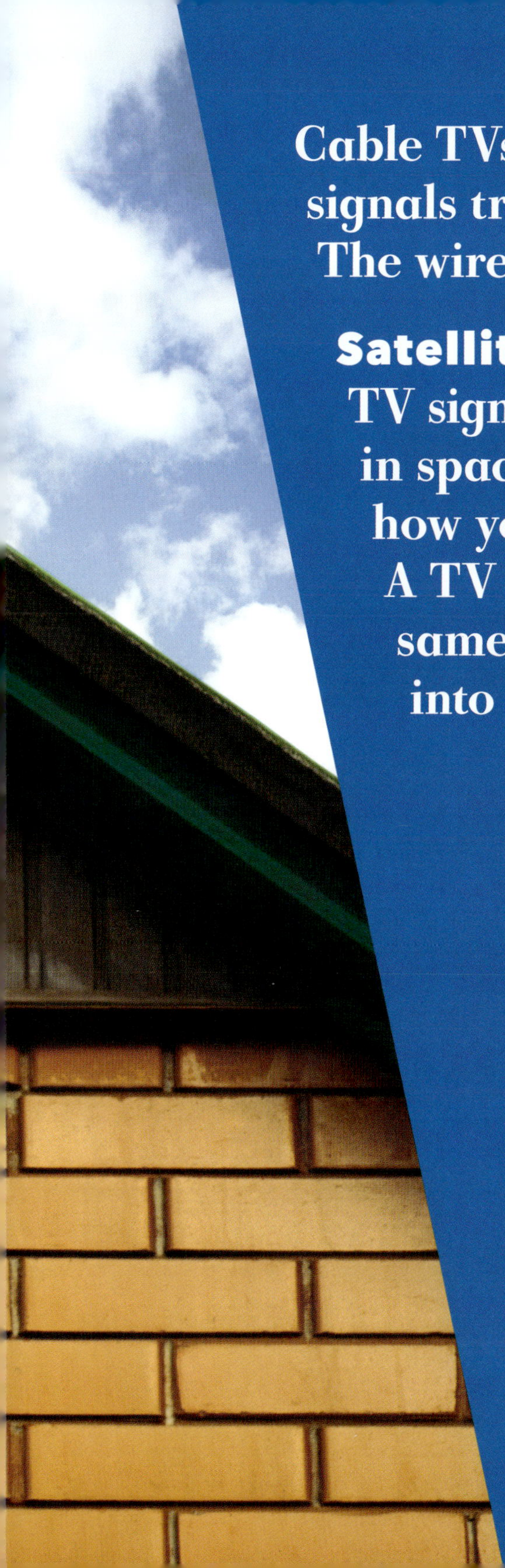

Cable TVs are different. Their signals travel through wires. The wires are underground.

Satellite dishes receive TV signals from a satellite in space. It doesn't matter how your signal arrives. A TV uses all signals the same way. It turns them into pictures and sound.

CHAPTER 2

TYPES OF TVs

There are many kinds of TVs. Most modern TVs are smart. This means they connect to the internet.

You can stream movies. You can play games. You can use apps, too. But TVs started out much simpler.

The first TVs sold on a large scale used **cathode ray tubes** (CRTs). CRT TVs became popular in the 1930s. A CRT is a glass tube. It is shaped like a funnel. A CRT TV gets a signal. The TV separates it into red, green, and blue signals. There is one **electron gun** for each color. These make beams of **electrons** that form the picture on the screen.

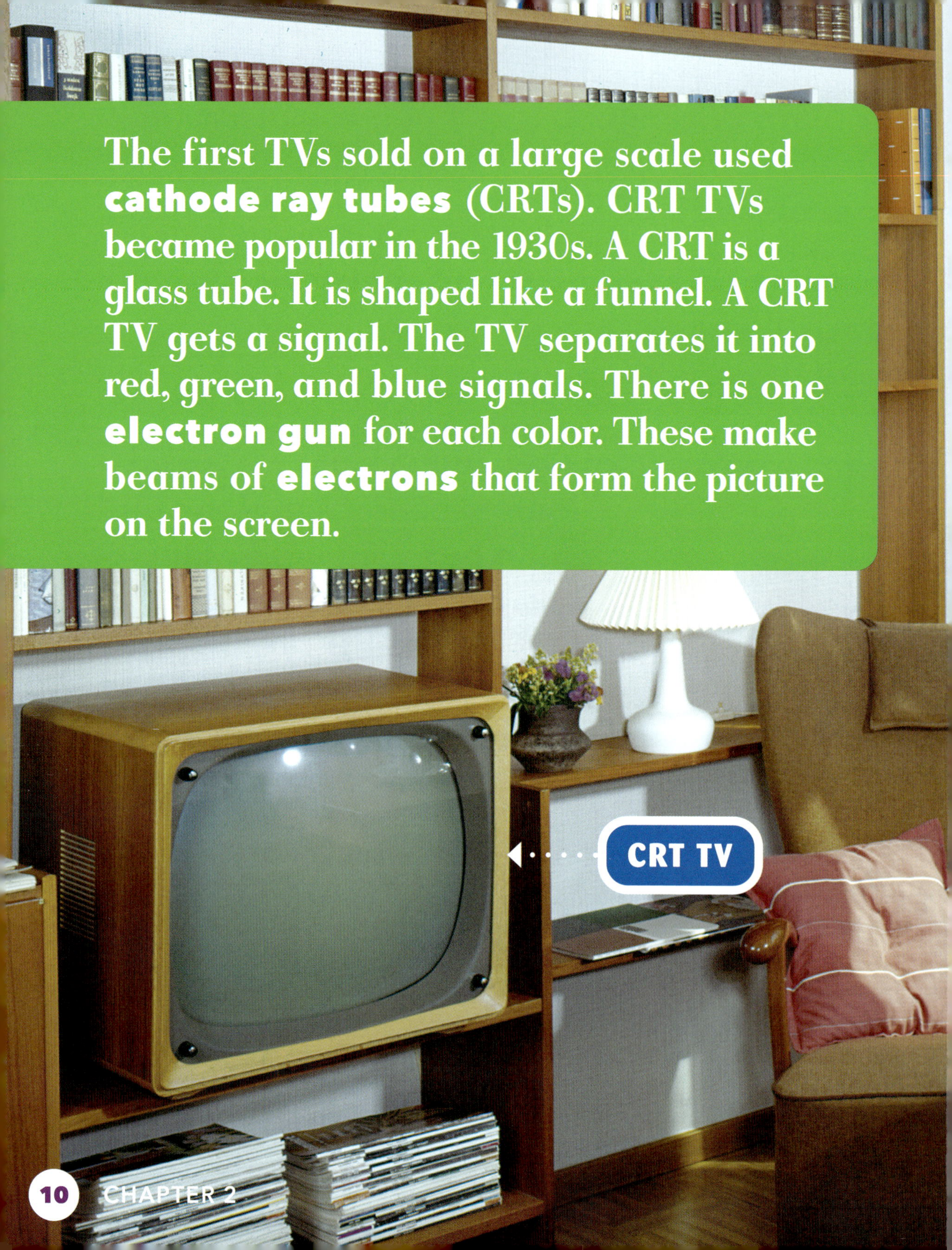

TAKE A LOOK!

How does a CRT TV work? Take a look!

1. **Electron guns send beams to a screen.**
2. **Dots on the screen glow red, green, or blue.**
3. **These dots form pictures on the TV screen.**

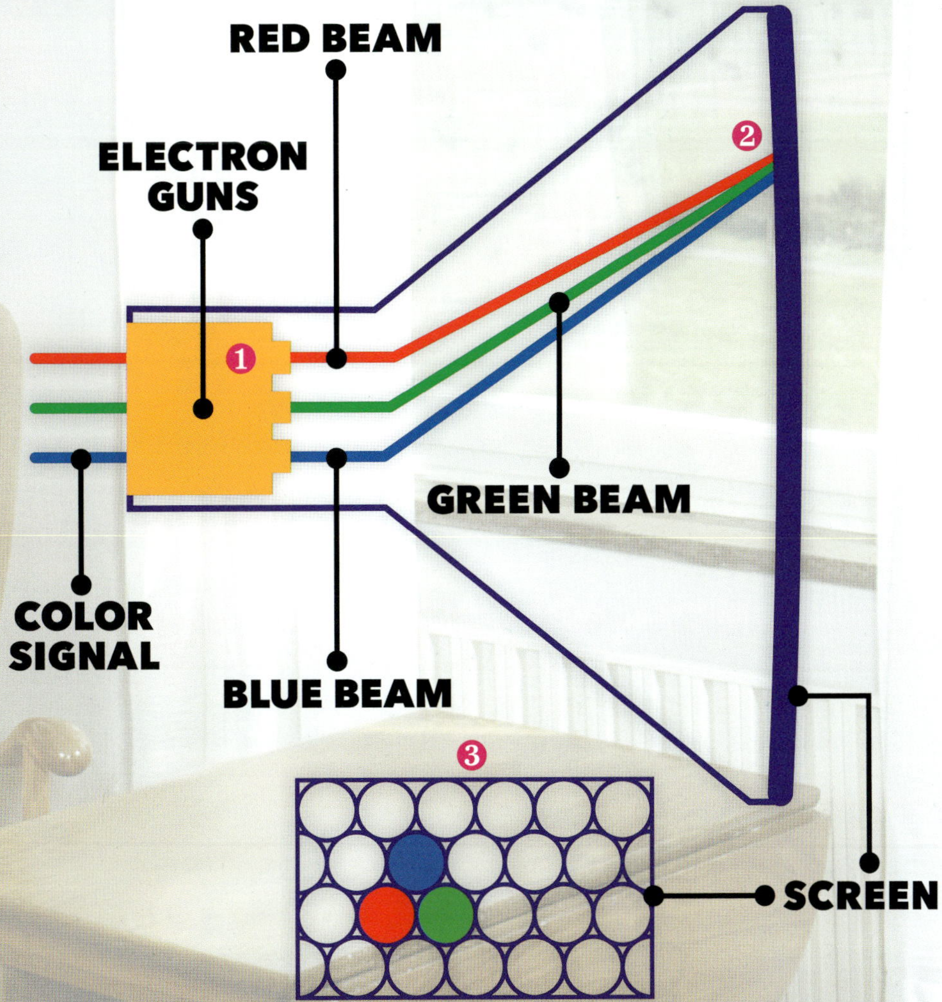

Most TVs today have flat screens. Why? They don't have a CRT. We call them flat-screen TVs.

Plasma TVs are one kind. Their screens are made up of gas cells. **Electric currents** run through the gas. Light **photons** are released. Each **pixel** glows red, green, or blue when photons hit it.

DID YOU KNOW?

Pixels are tiny dots of light. They form pictures on modern TV screens. The more pixels there are, the clearer the picture will be.

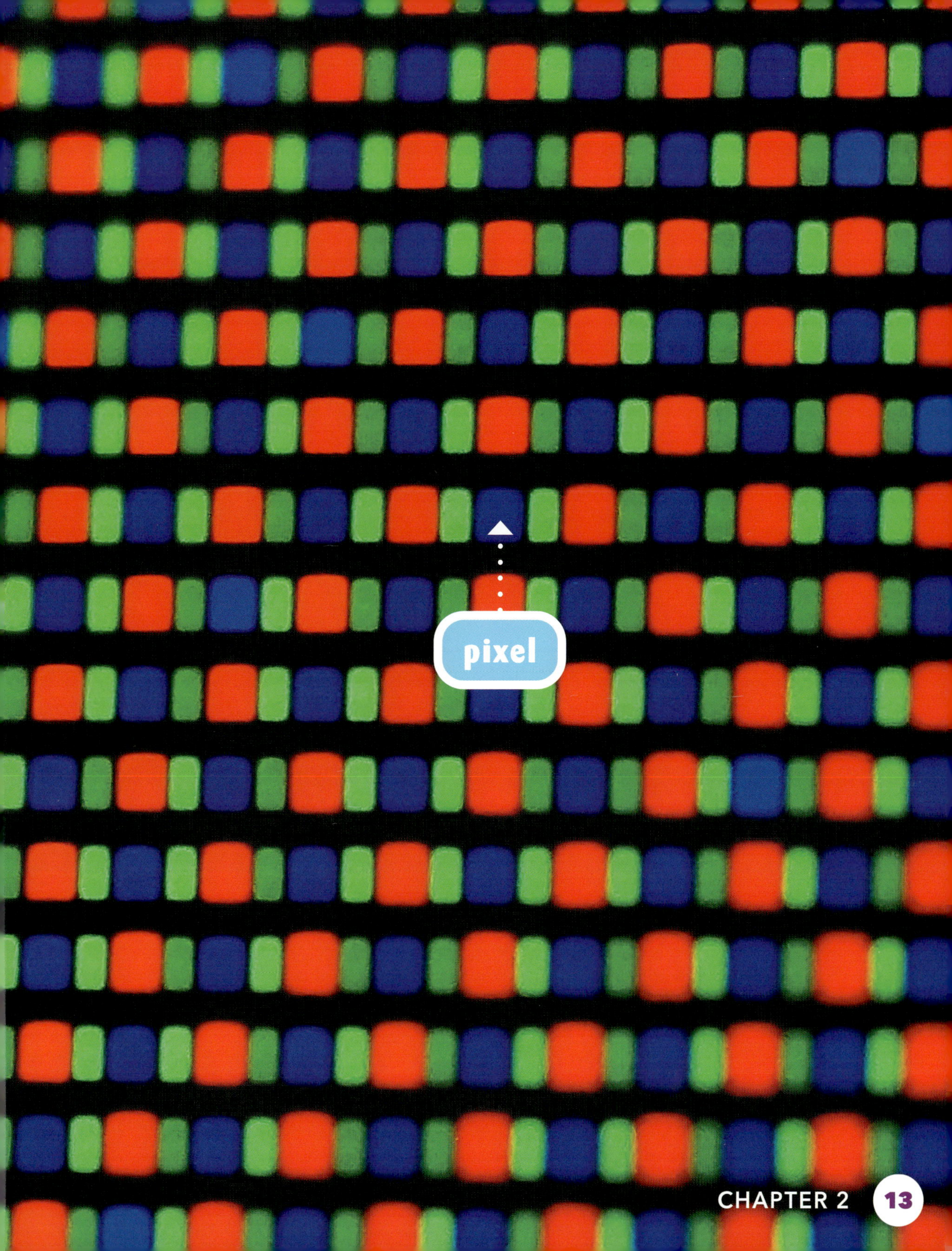
pixel

LCD TV

Liquid crystal display (LCD) screens are slim, too. Liquid crystal is made up of liquid with some solids. **Fluorescent** light is sent through it. An electric current is, too. It causes the solids to move. These block some light beams. They let other beams through.

LED TVs are a type of LCD. They use **light-emitting diodes** (LEDs). LED TVs are thinner than LCDs. Why? LED bulbs are smaller than fluorescent bulbs. LED screens provide a better picture, too.

DID YOU KNOW?

In 2006, LED TVs became more popular than plasma TVs. Why? LEDs were cheaper. They had thinner screens. They used less power. Some plasma TVs had a problem. Pictures burned into the screens. As of 2014, these TVs were no longer made.

CHAPTER 3

REMOTE CONTROLS

Before remote controls were **invented**, TVs were controlled by knobs.

Most remote controls have buttons. What happens when you press one? It sends pulses of **infrared** light to the TV. These pulses tell the TV to turn on and off. They change the volume. They change channels, too.

TVs have changed a lot since the 1930s. **Holographic** TVs could be made in the future. They could create 3D images. What ideas do you have for TVs of the future?

DID YOU KNOW?

Companies are working on TV screens that can bend. They are also working on screens that can roll up like window blinds.

ACTIVITIES & TOOLS

TRY THIS!

MAKE A TV TIMELINE

Technology has come a long way since TVs were first invented. Let's find out when improvements were made.

What You Need:

- a computer, tablet, or phone with internet access
- paper
- a pencil
- a ruler
- markers, crayons, or colored pencils

1. **Get permission from a parent or guardian to search the internet.**
2. **Research the history of television online. Write down the dates of important advances in television technology. When was each kind of television introduced?**
3. **Using paper, a pencil, and a ruler, create a timeline of these important dates. Use markers, crayons, or colored pencils to decorate your timeline.**

GLOSSARY

cathode ray tubes: Vacuum tubes that project electron beams onto a phosphor-coated screen to produce glowing color.

electric currents: Flows of electricity.

electron gun: A device in a cathode ray tube that emits beams of electrons.

electrons: The smallest particles within atoms.

fluorescent: A type of light that is very bright and usually shaped like a tube.

holographic: Of or relating to a projected 3D image.

infrared: Producing or using rays of light that are outside the visible spectrum of light.

invented: Produced for the first time.

light-emitting diodes: Sources that give off light when currents flow through them.

photons: Basic units of light.

pixel: The smallest graphic unit that can be shown on a digital display.

radio waves: Forms of electromagnetic radiation that can be used in communications such as radio, mobile phones, and television.

satellite: A spacecraft that is sent into orbit around Earth, the moon, or another heavenly body.

signals: Sounds, messages, or images that are transmitted.

transmitters: Equipment used to send waves carrying messages or signals.

INDEX

TO LEARN MORE

Finding more information is as easy as 1, 2, 3.

1. Go to www.factsurfer.com
2. Enter "TVsandremotecontrols" into the search box.
3. Choose your book to see a list of websites.

FACT SURFER